Running Your Finances

Applying the disciplines of long-distance running to your finances

Jeffrey Sartori

© 2020 Running Your Finances

ISBN: 9798584012656

All written content in this book is for information purposes only. Opinions provided are solely those of the author, unless otherwise specifically cited. All information or ideas provided should be discussed in detail with an advisor.

The information provided in this book is for informational purposes only and is not intended to be a source of advice or credit analysis with respect to the material presented. The information and/or documents contained in this book do not constitute legal or financial advice and should never be used without first consulting with a financial professional to determine what may be best for your individual needs.

Dedication

This book is dedicated to my beautiful wife, Betsy, who has believed in me and supported me along our journey. I am grateful to have such a wonderful partner who has unconditionally loved me through our peaks and valleys.

RUNNING
YOUR FINANCES

APPLYING THE DISCIPLINES
OF LONG-DISTANCE RUNNING
TO YOUR FINANCES

JEFFREY SARTORI

"Running Your Finances is a straightforward book for anyone who wants to achieve long-term financial success. Whether you're a runner or not you will quickly see the parallels of what it takes to focus on the long game for your life. Financial independence awaits you if you follow this book's advice slowly but surely."

- Todd Romer - Founder of Young Money University

Table of Contents

INTRODUCTION 1

1: GOAL SETTING 4

2: PLAYING THE LONG GAME 9

3: OWNERSHIP 18

4: MONITOR YOUR PROGRESS 24

5: HYDRATE REGULARLY 31

6: HAVE A RUNNING BUDDY 39

7: SLOW AND STEADY WINS THE RACE 43

8: DELAYED GRATIFICATION 48

9: FINAL LAP 58

AFTERWORD 61

Introduction

This book is the result of many years striving to be debt-free, becoming debt-free and pursuing financial independence. I have two driving passions in my life, personal finance and long-distance running. Although I have had these two passions for some time, they did not intersect until recently.

I began teaching a personal finance class in early 2018. While doing my training runs on the crushed limestone trails of the Cuyahoga Valley National Park, I worked on finance class topics. I have always worked through various scenarios, situations, and relational issues as I ran, but never made the connection between running disciplines and managing finances.

What I am offering here is for you to learn these disciplines to stay the course, no matter what your financial or running goals may be. I will encourage you, coach you and hopefully make you think about the life choices in front of you. I'll provide links, data, and ideas on finances, debt, budgeting, investing and running. My hope is that you will be encouraged to play the long game.

Let's start off by stating that I am not financially independent (FI) yet, but I'm well on the path to getting there! If you haven't started yet, or need help getting off the tarmac, I am reminded of a line from the Grateful Dead song *'Fire on the Mountain,'* "Long distance runner, what you standin' there for? Get up, get out, get out of the door."

Want to make your finances stronger? Apply the time-tested disciplines of running to managing your money.

I'll tackle each discipline throughout this book to draw out the comparisons between long distance running and managing money.

To get the most out of this book and to help out your future self, I encourage you to do the exercises after each chapter. Having a notebook where you congregate your answers may help with learning and applying the disciplines so you can review later and adjust your behavior as needed.

Running your finances is not rocket science. There are only a few steps one must learn and apply to run them successfully. Let's get off to a running start so you can

Introduction

finally take control of your money and your future. I thank you for allowing me the opportunity to share my insight on these key disciplines. Join me in living debt-free and within your means while playing the long game.

1

Goal Setting

"8% of people achieve their New Year's goals, with 92% failing."

– 2018 Statistic Brain Research Institute Goal Study

Over the last 20 years of my running passion, I have found that I will skip training workouts or have less of a desire to run if I do not have a "paid for" race lined up. Kinda weird, I know, but what does this mean?

It simply means that I need to put some money on the line and sign-up for a race in order to "motivate" me to continue race training. Paying $75 for a half-marathon entry fee or $45 for a 10K fee forces me to set a goal. The goal being that I will train vigorously for the upcoming race so that I receive a return on my investment! Maybe you need to sign-up for a gym membership for motivation or perhaps just purchasing a new pair of running shoes will motivate you.

"Where there is no vision, the people perish" **-Psalm 29:18** (Without a goal I will perish.)

Zig Zigler says, "If you aim at nothing, you will hit it every time." Once I pay my entry fee, my goal is in front of me and I know what I need to do each day/week to prepare for the upcoming race months away. Being frugal, I don't want to waste the money.

How does this relate to finances? I challenge you to find a successful person or a person who retired early that achieved it without a goal. My guess is that you won't find one because they don't exist.

Financial goals are no different from running goals. Setting a financial goal is a necessity to guiding one's focus and aim. Why save for the future if you don't know what you are saving for? When my kids were teens, we set up three envelopes for them to split up their babysitting money. It was a simple distribution: 80% savings, 10% giving, 10% spending. My daughter asked me why she has to put *all* of her money into the savings envelope. We then proceeded to talk about her savings goals which included a car for when she got out of college, and a new Yamaha keyboard or an iPhone. She really wanted the keyboard and knew it cost $600, so she could tangibly see her progress as she regularly deposited money into her savings envelope.

By linking a tangible goal to the savings envelope, my daughter *directed* her focus onto the *why*.

Ask yourself this question: What's your long-term savings goal? Maybe you don't have one because you are 20, 25, or 30 years away from retiring. Even though retirement may be a long way off, defining retirement, as it relates to you, will be an important first step.

What is Retirement?
Is it playing golf every day? Traveling whenever you want? Doing nothing? Working on your hobby? Maybe it is more altruistic and you want to volunteer your time? Or perhaps you want the freedom to do what you want and not have to go through the daily grind?

I define retirement as not having to be beholden to a 9-5 job to meet my living expenses. I do not believe work ceases at retirement. Working is part of who we are, whether it be daily exercise, volunteering, pursuing a

Goal Setting

hobby, land lording, consulting or mentoring younger folks.

No matter what "retirement" means to you, you'll need to "finance" it. Funding your retirement won't just happen without a plan. The government is not going to provide you with all of your needs and wants. It's up to you.

Once you've determined your long-term savings goal, calculate how much savings you will need to fund your retirement. We will cover this in depth later in the book.

Did you notice I am using phrases like "fund it" and "finance it"? This is to help you think of yourself as the owner of your retirement. Who else would own your retirement? You are the captain of your ship. No one else.

The first financial discipline is taking time to slowly write down your long-term savings goals. Your goals needs to be actionable and reviewed on a routine basis.

Exercise:

- Write down some things you want to fund in your life?
- Write down your financial goals. Then for one week, review and revise these goals daily. This daily exercise will help define and sharpen what you want to achieve.
- Define what retirement is to you.
- Determine if you are a saver or spender.

Self-Reflection:

- Take time to think what is it you really want after all of your years of working?

2

Playing the Long Game

To save or to spend, that is the question.

Every runner knows that pain is coming. It's not a matter of if, but when. Without a plan, an inexperienced runner will just give in to the pain. Non-runners won't even start because of the fear of the pain.

In order to overcome the bumps, twangs, and exhaustion of a jarring run, I need a running plan of what I am going to do today. As the motivational speaker and ex-Navy Seal Chad Wright says, "Quitting is not an option." He takes the option of quitting off the table. Either his body will collapse or he's crossing the finish line by himself. That's determination. That's goal setting. That's a plan.

What is a runner's pain management tool? It's the planned goal set prior to the run. Being prepared. One of my favorite pain management tools is projecting my thoughts into the future to how I will feel when I finish the run. My goal is to look at my race time and feel good about what I accomplished.

That's success. That's playing the long game.

Here's the truth. If you are a would-be half-marathoner or marathoner, you will need to stick to your endurance training plan for weeks to learn to cope with discomfort for extended periods of time. Newsflash: there is no short-cut to building endurance. You need to start today! Each week you delay is compromising your future.

I'll put my coach's hat on and give you another hard pill to swallow. There will be pain, not just discomfort, in the beginning. If your training only consists of random jogging spurts, you'll never complete a marathon. At some point, you need to make the mental transition from jogging to running.

Similarly, if you're only saving 2-5% for retirement, you can consider yourself a jogger. You might rationalize, "At least I am saving something." The truth is, however, that at a jogging rate you will be working a long, long time before you can actually retire. The bigger the effort, the better the gain. In other words, short-term pain now means you won't be a greeter at Walmart when you are 65. Unless, of course, that is your definition of retirement. A general rule of thumb for beginners is to save at least 15% of your gross income for long-term savings. 15% won't get you to financial independence quickly, but you will be starting a good habit of savings.

A quick example to free-up additional monies for savings. Let's say you currently buy your lunch every day for $8/day. You then decide to make a change and pack your lunch. As a result you save about $25/week after you pay for groceries. If you are 22-year-old and save $25/week until the age of 62, you will have amassed $278,000 at a 7% return. That return comes from saving only $100/month. Imagine saving even more than $25/week.

Every runner needs to determine when to save energy and when to expend energy during a run.

When I am running and I see a hill approaching, I immediately begin to think about conserving energy so that I can make it up the hill and not stop while trying. I am consciously making a decision not to spend energy now so that I am able to supply (or spend) energy in the future when I really need it. If I prematurely choose to "hit the boosters" and pick up my pace, chances are high that I will run out of gas and not finish the race or have a very poor performance.

Another example is when I am driving my Toyota Prius. I am addicted to watching the ECO Monitor to see if I am pulling energy from the Hybrid battery or from gasoline. Naturally, I try to coast as much as possible and use the regenerative brakes for as long as possible to save on fuel. I truly love it when I am driving on the highway and cars or trucks are flying past me. *Chic Ching* – it's the sound of making money. Music to my ears, albeit only a few dollars less at the pump, but still a few dollars ahead by conserving and thinking longer term.

In the finance world, we call this "opportunity cost." This is an interesting concept and one worth understanding. When we purchase an item now, we pass on the opportunity to purchase other items later. We are foregoing future opportunities. Opportunity cost is what we give up in the future to have what we want now. If you want to drive fast now, you'll have to give up more dollars later at the pump.

For example, if you have a typical new car payment of $534 for the car "you couldn't live without", that same

$534 <u>cannot</u> be used to fund your long-term savings goals, travel, or your car replacement fund.

Opportunity costs are neither good nor bad, it's just what they are. It is the price you pay to have NOW what you want now. Most people probably think they will always have a car payment and that it's just a way of life. These folks are more interested in driving an expensive, newer car in the present versus driving a reliable, USED car now and re-allocating car payment monies for longer-term financial goals.

To save or to spend?

What drives you to spend or to save? Do you consider yourself a spender or a saver? Have you heard of the "Need vs. Want" discussion? Many things we think we "need" are really just "wants" and not necessities. I really need a Starbucks coffee this morning. I am buying a new car because I need a reliable car. I need this sweet, new Patagonia jacket for winter.

Now before you ditch this idea, please understand that I love great coffee, sweet rides and excellent gear. But I refrain from buying everything new and at full price. Do I have to have a coffee shop boil the water and grind the beans for my coffee? No. I enjoy awesome, locally-roasted fair-trade, organic coffee for a fraction of the price. How do I do this? I plan ahead to appease my cravings (or...I appease my cravings by planning ahead). Planning ahead is another discipline that runners take into the personal finance world.

Can a used car be reliable? Absolutely! But you have to do your homework. Is buying a new car a *need* or a *want*? We Americans like to convince ourselves that there is too much risk in buying used cars, even if it's certified. Convincing ourselves is just a sham so that we don't have to look into the future.

With that said, if you are a millionaire, go buy the new car since that purchase will not be changing the course of your finances and your budget can actually afford it. But then again, if you ARE a millionaire, you probably have already been buying used cars and will continue to do so, as that is one of the reasons you were able to become a millionaire and avoid car debt. A great book on this concept is The Millionaire Next Door[1] by Thomas J Stanley.

---

[1] https://www.amazon.com/Millionaire-Next-Door-Surprising-Americas/dp/1589795474

Playing the Long Game

Choosing to save now vs. spend now clearly takes discipline, fortitude, and motivation. It is paramount that you recognize whether your intended purchase is a need or a want. If it is a need, have you researched the best price alternatives? If it is truly just a want, then does your budget allow you to purchase the item?

As you can see, it is a daily activity to determine if my next purchase is a need or want. How much am I spending in opportunity cost currency? If you think like you're the owner of your money, then you will want to make a profit at the end of the year. Your long-term savings would be considered your profit. For instance, having a large house, fancy car, or a boat, all highly-leveraged, gives the illusion of wealth, but is not true wealth. True wealth is what you don't spend and the monies you still have in your possession, not what you buy.

In addition to long-term savings, each of us has monthly spending that occurs whether it is written down or not. For instance, a relative or close friend's birthday is coming up or you want to go rent kayaks for a couple hours to enjoy the outdoors. There will always be birthdays, entertainment, and spur of the moment ideas that need money to fund them. But do you know if you truly have the money for this activity? These are not expensive purchases, but you still need to have the money to purchase them. If I know that I want to rent kayaks this weekend, I may go easy on my trip to the grocery store, Target or Costco. Playing the long game means you are suited up and playing the game and not on the sidelines "thinking" about saving or playing the ostrich by ignoring life. Go ahead and rent the kayaks, just make sure you have the cash.

You will need some tools to know if you have enough money for your long-term savings plan at the end of the month. We will discuss these tools in the following chapters.

Are you ready to play the long game?

Exercise:

- At what age would you like to retire?
- What is your long-term savings goal?
- How much money will you need to finance your goal?
- What is your plan to reach your long-term goal?
- What are the main roadblocks stopping you?
- Evaluate your purchases this coming week and see if you are purchasing because of needs or wants.

Self-Reflection:

- Do I need to commit to a less expensive lifestyle?
- What needs to change in my life to have a "plan ahead mentality?"

3

Ownership

"O Captain! My Captain! Rise up and hear the bells."

- Walt Whitman

A few days ago, I headed to work out at lunchtime but approached the treadmill with no real goal. Guess what happened? I wasn't really motivated and I only ran 1.5 miles before stopping. Not that I was super tired or injured, just not motivated. Has that happened to you?

Then today I headed to the gym for a run, again at lunchtime, and something different happened. I remembered my lackluster attempt at working out a few days prior, so I set a goal prior to walking into the gym. I told myself that I would run 3.1 miles, period. Boom! Instantaneous goal. I also had the memory of the disappointing performance that I did not want to repeat. It worked. I had a great run and did not consider stopping at the 1-

Ownership

mile mark, 2-mile mark or even the 2.5-mile mark. There was no wavering.

The whole premise of playing the long game in long-distance running or in running your personal finances is to play. You need to be on the team to play the long game. Not a spectator. Playing the game is having a plan. Planning ahead. Owning the plan.

Who owns your finance plan?

Do you have a plan for how you will meet your long-term savings goal? If the answer is no, then why not? Is it too overwhelming? Will it take too long to accumulate that much money?

Here's a simple truth. It takes everyone a long time. There is no quick path, sorry. Even if you are a hyper-saver and saving 50-60% of your income, it will still take multiple years to reach financial independence.

Nothing great happens by accident.

Let me say that again: nothing happens by accident, especially the accumulation of wealth.

When you have a plan and execute your plan, you still need to consistently remind yourself "why" you're not spending NOW. The pulls of society and slick corporate marketing campaigns are so strong that we need an opposite, equally-strong pull to play the long game.

What has Superman strength to do this?

Your mind.

Here is the paradigm shift that needs to happen in your mind, moving from victim-mentality to owner-mentality. You need to be engaged. Be the owner.

Simply stated, you need to own YOUR plan.

I've said it before, you are the captain of your ship. Not the government. Not your employer. Not a potential inheritance. Just you!

If you agree with this concept, then from this point forward you are owning the management of your money.

Ring the bell, O Captain! The pace you set now for saving money will determine the final timeline for reaching your long-term savings goal.

Time can be your friend or your enemy.

Ownership

Your pace for savings has a lot to do with your age and how much longer you need to work in a "daily grind" capacity. Naturally, if you are younger, your savings pace can be slower than if you are older since a younger person has more time for pacing.

Can you start saving money now? Could you live on your current salary each year for the next ten years while saving any raises, bonuses or side-hustle money that comes your way? Sure you could, BUT do you want to? Is the sacrifice worth it?

When I was training to complete my 5k lunchtime run, I had to push through the pain, discomfort and constant desire to quit in order to reach my goal. I took a page from Chad Wright's playbook and took quitting off the table as a short-term option. I decided to sacrifice and apply grit to reach my lunchtime workout goal of running the 5k.

As far as determining long-term savings goals, online retirement calculators can be very helpful. For simple math, let's say you want $1,000,000 US dollars saved for retirement. Once you hit $1 million, you will quit your daily grind job. There are lots of retirement calculators on the web to choose from. An easy retirement calculator is found on Bankrate.[2]

This calculator will give you an idea of how much you still need to save to reach your goal. By using a tool like this, you are taking ownership of managing your money. Congratulations.

If you're acting like an owner, you get to decide if you want to save or spend every day. No more blaming or passing the buck.

Exercise:

- Determine if your long-term goal is more important than short-term pleasures.
- This upcoming week, make note if you have grit and push through obstacles or if you take the easy road of quitting.
- What are the main roadblocks stopping you from achieving your long-term success?

---

[2] https://www.bankrate.com/retirement/calculators/retirement-plan-calculator/

Ownership

Self-Reflection:

- What barriers are stopping me from being the owner of my money?
- Do you think you will remember the short-term pain of sacrifice in the future? Will you remember the sting from the sacrifice? Or the reward of making the sacrifice?

4

Monitor Your Progress

Excuse me Mr. Budget, can I buy a cup of coffee today? The entertainment category is empty, so "No!" If you disregard, then you will be in deeper debt to General MasterCard longer. Enjoy the Jo.

Let's take a look at a scenario. I am in the middle of my training run...sweating, checking my Garmin[3] for pace and distance, and deciding my next move. I quickly assess how I feel and determine if I have enough energy to reach today's running goal. I am able to regulate my speed based on how much energy is in my tank and how much further I have to run to reach my goal.

Based on past performance, I know that if I spend too much energy on a hill or sprint, my pace will suffer later in my run when my energy level will not be sufficient. By

---

[3] https://www.garmin.com/en-US/

Monitor your Progress

keeping a close watch on my energy output, I can guarantee I'll meet my goal, provided there is not an emergency situation.

There are so many benchmarking apps for Smartphones that it's dizzying. I am a Garmin guy, so that's my tool of choice. They have a great Garmin Connect[4] app that has everything needed to monitor my performance progress or degradation.

Any serious runner monitors their performance, especially during training runs. This is when a runner can make adjustments to his or her tempo. During a live race, each runner's performance is based on all of their training leading up to the big race.

Much like burning energy when I run, I also "burn" or spend money in pre-allocated spending categories. In creating a monthly spending plan, I pre-determine how much I am able to spend per category. I give every dollar a purpose. I am the owner. I give the orders to my money.

Do you know if you can "afford" that new iPhone? Or a weekend trip?

---

[4] https://connect.garmin.com/

Running Your Finances

What can you afford to spend?

Here are some mechanics.

Before we can determine how much you can spend on a new cell phone or weekend travel, we must build a monthly budget or spending plan. A budget is simply pre-determining how much money a person can spend per spending category.

I have been teaching Budgeting 101 for several years and I have yet to find an easier way other than the old-fashioned tracking method.

You will need to track your expenses for 30-60 days. The easiest way to do this is log every money transaction that you make, each day. My blog site provides a downloadable expense tracking sheet. I know it's a pain in the bottom, but there really is no better way to look at the details behind your spending.

Some folks ask for a receipt after every transaction then log the receipts every evening, while others track the expenses on an Excel spreadsheet. Or if you do all transactions via debit card or credit card, you can review each evening and log what was spent. Don't forget the auto-withdrawals that appear on your bank statement, as each

Monitor your Progress

of these withdrawals count as transactions and need to be logged (i.e. Netflix fee, gym membership, insurance premium, etc.)

If you can project your thoughts 30-60 days into the future, you can expect a tangible log of all the money that you deposited into your account as well as all the money that was spent.

The next four steps are fairly straight-forward:

1. At the end of each 30-day period, ask yourself a question: Do I have a surplus of money or did I have to borrow from long-term savings or a credit card?
2. Each money transaction should be categorized into a Spending Category (i.e. rent, utilities, groceries, entertainment, car payment, fuel, savings, etc.) If you have debt, include credit card payments, student loans, personal loans, or any other loan.
3. After each transaction is categorized, sum all the transactions per category. These categories will become the basis of your monthly budget.
4. Determine your net income (after taxes) on a monthly basis. Make sure to count paychecks, tips,

and all miscellaneous income. This is the money you have to work with to determine how much you can spend.

The world likes telling us to "buy now and pay later," but as a coach, I am asking you, "Who would you want advising you how to spend your hard-earned money?" Your budget or a random corporate marketing campaign? Don't believe the lie that says you can buy whatever you want now and pay for it tomorrow. Will you be able to pay for it tomorrow? At what cost? Will you ever reach your long-term savings goal if you continue to make purchases today using tomorrow's money?

There's always a cost.

Again, the #1 running discipline is goal setting. The #1 personal finance discipline is goal setting.

What can you focus on to pull you towards the long game versus towards gratifying immediate short-term desires? A simple budget that you actually want to follow, which also shows your progress.

If you only have $40 for entertainment for the weekend then you **only have $40** for entertainment and not $100. Live within your means; don't spend money you really

Monitor your Progress

don't have. Living like someone you are not gets expensive. If you have a big event coming in a few weeks, then you should save your $40 entertainment dollars for a few weeks so that you would amass $120 over 3 weeks for your big event. This is great – no more guessing! It is satisfying to know your exact weekly entertainment budget.

There are many tools on the internet to assist you with generating a budget, so my goal is not to reproduce what has already been done. I am a fan of YNAB[5] (You Need A Budget), Mint[6] or using an Excel sheet to track. The exciting part of generating a spending plan or budget is seeing how much money you're able to allocate to your long-term savings goal. Unfortunately, if there is no money left over at the end of the month, you cannot fund your future.

Just as a runner monitors their running progress, you will need to track your daily expenses so you know how much "fuel" you have to fund your long-term savings goal.

Exercise:

---

[5] https://www.youneedabudget.com/
[6] https://www.mint.com

- Track your expenses for a 30 day period, and then an additional 30 days, for a two month total. Include any auto withdrawals from your checking account.
- After 60 days, categorize your money transactions.

Self-Reflection:

- Ask yourself this question: are you living like someone who has more disposable income than you do?
- Are you living above your means?

5

Hydrate Regularly

Maintaining hydration as a runner is important for health while improving recovery, minimizing injury, and maximizing performance.

-Brigham Health Hub

An hour before a training run, I try to drink about 16 ounces of water so my body is properly hydrated. Once I consume this initial hydration, my body is set. If a training run is longer than one hour, then I will bring some Gatorade in a small bottle that fits into my Adalid Hydration Belt.[7] If I don't hydrate during the long runs as well as immediately after, my body will not respond well to heat exhaustion and lack of fluids.

---

[7] https://adalidgear.com/

After runs, I continue hydrating with regular water or Electrolyte water. Some runners are now hydrating with cold tea. Throughout a normal day, runners will drink lots of water because we know that water is key to flushing toxins and replenishing fluids. But it takes a plan to continue drinking water.

At first, it really took me some effort to drink 32 ounces of water a day, as my bio-breaks greatly increased. As you can imagine, sometimes I just don't feel like drinking more water. When these feelings arise, I look back to my goal. I want to be healthy so I can successfully complete the paid-for race I have planned.

Take a gulp my friend.

Again, I am going back to the goal I set. Since I am playing for the long game, I will forego the immediate desire to not drink anymore water.

Why am I talking about hydrating before, during and after running? The reason is because much like running, our finances need constant hydration. A few ways we can hydrate our finances are regular deposits into our savings, investments or retirement accounts.

Hydrate Regularly

There's a cool concept out there called Dollar Cost Averaging (DCA). The DCA concept tells us to make regular deposits into a retirement account, no matter what the stock market is doing. It does not take into account market fluctuations. It's a wonderful concept to setup. First, you pre-determine the amount you want to save for retirement. Second, you have your employer or investment company (i.e. Vanguard) automatically withdraw your pre-determined amount on a weekly, bi-weekly or monthly time table.

I call it money management hydration.

Having it automatic is key, as our human emotions can get in the way and want to divert this money. I know Murphy will come knocking on your door. He likes to visit me as well. Besides doing DCA for my retirement account, I also set aside 4 months of living expenses into an Emergency Fund as a short-term savings goal. When Murphy knocks, I open the door to my Emergency Fund and do not sweat it. To get 4 months of expenses saved, I had to regularly deposit money into my high-yield savings account. I currently use the platform Synchrony Bank.[8] You should save between 3-6 months living expenses, which is actually less

---

[8] https://www.synchronybank.com/

than 3-6 months of your income because if you are unemployed, you will not be paying taxes, making investments, funding savings or giving to charity.

When an emergency arises, you will need to withdraw from your Emergency Fund. You will cease all other savings goals and begin depositing back into your Emergency Fund. You will need to continue until it is fully funded again as this now becomes your #1 saving priority.

Once you have a fully-funded Emergency Fund, you'll realize it feels nice to be the bank.

The other hydration step is on the investment side. Provided you have a 401k, IRA, Roth IRA or SEP, you will need to incorporate a portfolio re-balance on a semi-annual basis. It's a simple concept. You pre-determine your investment asset allocation. Asset allocation is how you allocate your retirement money. You can allocate monies into stocks, bonds, real estate, gold, silver, oil, and many other areas.

As an example (this is not financial advice), I allocate over 85% to an S&P 500 mutual fund, 2.5% to an international growth fund, 2.5% to an intermediate-term bond fund, and 10% to a crowd-funding eREIT. I personally use

Hydrate Regularly

Vanguard low-cost funds when possible as they are in-expensive, well-established, and are the pioneer of the mutual fund industry. You will notice that I do not have a high percentage of bonds in my asset allocation. Since I am not planning on pulling all of my long-term savings out at once, I have time to wait out any market fluctuations. Even when another downturn comes, I will keep my allocation as-is since I am playing the long game and am not interested in chasing short-term trends. When I re-balance my investments, I go back to the goal I set and make sure the investments are still tracking to my goals. If not, then I will adjust as needed.

If you need assistance with asset allocation, I can recommend the book, 'All About Asset Allocation'[9] by Richard Ferri, which goes into detail on varying concepts and strategies. Additionally, you can go to the Vanguard asset allocation[10] website to preview their thoughts on asset mixes per asset class. My goal is not to give you investment strategies, but to help you think about this important step in the money management hydration process.

---

[9] https://www.amazon.com/All-About-Asset-Allocation-Second/dp/0071700781
[10] https://investor.vanguard.com/investing/investment/

To keep hydrating my long-term savings goal, I pay myself first. After paying taxes on my income, which is usually automatic, I fund my 401k, Roth IRA, Education 529 Plans, and Savings account. Another way to look at it is to fund your long-term savings first, then live off what is left over. Most folks that I have taught had been doing the opposite. They pay their expenses and debt first, then if anything is left over, they might put a few dollars aside. Unfortunately, this type of short-term thinking is prevalent among most people. I recently read that the median age to start saving is 40 years old (News, 2020). Wow! What have people been doing throughout their 20s and 30s? My guess it's that they have been thinking short-term to fund a certain lifestyle.

One of my goals for writing this book is to help folks make a turn in their thinking and realize that saving for their future is more important than maintaining a certain lifestyle.

It's worth mentioning here that if you do have debt, you will need a plan to tackle it head on. You will have a very hard time reaching your long-term savings goal if you have to continue to pay down debt. There is a creative

Hydrate Regularly

concept out there called **Debt Snowball**. NerdWallet[11] has an excellent Debt Snowball Calculator that I would recommend using as you eliminate your debt.

Let's define what debt is. Debt is any money that you owe another individual or institution. Typical debts are mortgage loans, student loans, automobile loans, personal loans, and credit card debt.

The Debt Snowball concept is to list all of your debts and the associated remaining balance, interest rate, and minimum payments. The calculator calculates when all the debt will be paid-off using the minimum payments. There is an accelerator where you can add extra money each month and the calculator will tell you how quickly you can be debt-free. I highly encourage you to use this calculator or one similar. I'm a big visual guy so when my wife and I were paying off debt, we created one of those goofy thermometers and put it on our fridge so we could get motivated. It was also a great conversation piece when friends and family came over as well.

---

[11] https://www.nerdwallet.com/article/finance/debt-snowball-calculator

Exercise:

- Become your own bank: Have a goal to save 3-6 months of living expenses as an emergency fund.
- Save a minimum of $1,000 as an emergency fund.
- Create a monthly budget based on your 60 days of tracking.
- Determine your investment asset allocation.

Self-Reflection:

- Do I truly want to be debt free?
- Is how I am living now being kind to my future self?

6

Have a Running Buddy

Studies have shown that strong support systems can often reduce stress, depression and anxiety. While negative people can drain your energy and bring you down.

Runners know injuries will come. It's not a matter of if, but when. I was recently on a jog in my neighborhood and at mile 2.5, I unexpectedly hit a pothole as I was watching for approaching cars. Just like that, I rolled my ankle. Ouch! I didn't break it, but it took me two weeks before I was back and running. I probably could have run sooner, but since I play the long game, the short-term desire to run sooner did not out-flash my goal to be running into my sixties.

Also, I was encouraged through the various running sites I visit, as well as through my running friends, to stay off my foot. Without this encouragement, I might have given in to my short-term desires.

By surrounding myself with people of like-mind, I was encouraged by their stories, wisdom and experience. I have learned that the most effective road to success is to surround myself with people who have already mastered what I want to accomplish and then learn from them. In endurance sports, this sometimes means joining running clubs or finding other bicycle riders to push you forward on those 50-mile weekend rides.

Having a team behind you to guide and motivate you is very valuable both in endurance sports and wealth building.

When my wife and I were in debt and trying to dig ourselves out, we routinely listened to financial advisor Dave Ramsey's podcast and got encouraged that we could do it. I can still remember hearing the couples who called in to the show giving their "Debt free scream." It was motivating! Exhilarating. You are not alone on this journey.

I am writing this book in the Fall of 2020 during COVID craziness. The stock market took an incredible 25% downturn in the March/April timeframe. Now in September,

Have a Running Buddy

the stock market has made gains beyond where it was at the beginning of the year. Hopefully, you were not one of the folks who sold your mutual funds when the market was in a downfall and the media was selling negativity like it was candy. If you were, perhaps the negative influencers got to you. You could benefit from a support team as you determine to play the long game.

By having a support team, using key websites, consulting with financial advisors, and being a student of history, I didn't sell a thing. On the contrary, I continued my DCA and bought when the market was low. I followed the Sage of Omaha, Warren Buffet, as he says to be "fearful when others are greedy and greedy when others are fearful." I didn't touch my asset allocations or decrease my automatic withdraws into my retirement and savings accounts. I just continued working my plan and ignoring the noise.

Who do you have in your corner? Who is encouraging you? We all need a cheerleader or another human who has seen past the current pain you are experiencing. I ut groups. You need more. We all need encouragement as life does not always go as we planned.

News flash: Your car will need a repair. It's not a question of if, but when. Do you have an emergency fund ready to help you in times of need? Or will you go further in debt by using a credit card and paying the minimum? I'm ready for Murphy's visit, are you?

Exercise:

- Find several friends, bloggers, or websites that have your best interests at heart and want you to win at playing the long game.
- Tell one person, other than a family member, that you want to be debt-free.

Self-Reflection:

- Do I have a support team?
- Are there other folks in my life who are on a similar journey that I can connect with?

7

Slow and Steady Wins the Race

Does the hare ever beat the tortoise?

Running down a hill seems easy and natural. As you continue down the slope, it's easy to pick up speed and cruise. But is it wise? Running down a hill causes extra strain on one's thighs, hips and feet. It's ok to spend a little more energy and increase your speed naturally, but the temptation to really go fast is ever-present.

I was running one of my first half-marathons in Cleveland over a decade ago and there was a section where there was a good 2/10th of mile downhill. My pace was off, so I decided to hit the boosters as I ran down the hill. I was passing runners like it was nothing. I was flying. I could feel the pounding of the pavement against my feet and thighs as I increased my speed. As I reached the bottom, I was moving at a pretty fast clip. Then I noticed something.

Up ahead there was a hill. As I started up the hill, I began feeling pain in my legs and my lungs. As a result, my speed decreased. My head was down as I attempted to push up the hill. As I looked up, the same runners I had passed on the downhill were now over-taking me on the ascent. I couldn't believe it. I assumed I was way ahead of them. I really never recovered to catch those runners that ended-up passing me.

I remember the first half-marathon I ran – *The Buckeye Half* in the Cuyahoga Valley National Park. My running buddy, Doug, convinced me to run a *half*. I had no idea what to expect since I had never run in a long-distance race against other runners. My only goal was to finish. The gun sounded and the runners were off. This was pre-GPS days, so all I had was my *Timex Ironman* to check my pace. I went out blazingly fast because I felt great. Little did I know I was burning my reserves. I was the hare. By mile 10, I was toast and I still had a 5k to run. It was brutal and ugly, but somehow I finished. I learned a great lesson that morning. Pacing is your friend, not your enemy.

How does pacing relate to your personal finances? Let's first define what wealth is and is not. My definition of wealth is simply what you don't spend. Wealth cannot be measured by what a person earns. As one's earnings increase, the temptation to spend more increases at a faster rate.

When I spend my income on things I truly need and not on things I simply want, it takes discipline and determination. Spending more when your income rises is as tempting as running faster on a downhill or at the beginning of the race. The draw towards financial independence must be stronger than the desire to impress others by buying things.

How can a person cultivate a desire for financial independence? Is it a natural born discipline or can it be learned? It most certainly can be learned. Here is the best tool you can use to start becoming financially independent. Put constant, automatic and steady deposits into long-term savings. Let the initial decision to setup an automatic deposit be the anchor to keep you on track. Monthly subjectivity is eliminated as well as the draw to spend your budgeted long-term savings dollars. Naturally, the opportunity still exists to purchase *status* items by stopping your automatic deposit, but you will have made it more difficult for your future self.

Building wealth is not necessarily about earning more. Clearly there is nothing wrong with increasing your salary and gaining higher investment returns, but these are not guarantees to wealth. As your earnings increase and that increase is being offset by additional spending, then you haven't gained any ground in the wealth department. You've probably gained some ground in the status area. Congratulations.

Do you want status or wealth?

I have found that my decision to be financially independent outweighs the desire for status. Do I need this year's Topo's Magnifly shoe model? That would be sweet, but the truth is, a new pair of last year's model is just fine. I can certainly find websites that have an overstock, maybe it's not my preferred color, but who cares? Do I care more about the color of my running shoes or that I am saving 50% off last year's model's price?

I know which I will choose. How about you?

Does the hare ever beat the tortoise? Last time I checked, the tortoise still won.

Exercise:

- Determine the maximum amount you can allocate to long-term savings.
- Set up automatic deposits into your long-term savings vehicles.

Self-Reflection:

- Am I more concerned with status or building wealth?
- By earning more money, will I reach my long-term savings goal?

8

Delayed Gratification

Merriam-Webster's definition of wealth: an abundance of valuable possessions or money.

Running in the heat causes one to lose focus on the goal. I am constantly battling myself on long morning runs in early August when it's already in the 80s. I bargain with myself about when I can take my next sip of water. If I drink too much, too early, I will either get a cramp or not have any water left over when I really need it.

To solve this dilemma, I determine to delay my immediate desire for water. I pre-set water drinking intervals, which conserves my water supply while also encouraging contentment. I push through the pain of thirst knowing that I will have another sip in 15 minutes. Although the thirst may become stronger, I can continue running confidant in the clear-headed decisions made prior to my run. I trust myself. I trust the system I put in place to keep me on track.

Much like setting up automatic deposits and living on the money that's left over, I become content with the journey I am on. A strange thing happens when contentment enters the picture. As I become content with living on less, my income actually grows as I am not spending more than I need. I think it's actually easier to live with less than to try and grow my income.

What I am talking about is lifestyle. The learning curve to live on less than what you make is an extremely easy concept to understand. Understanding it and mastering it are two different skills.

With running, I need to build tolerance to resist running too fast downhill or not drinking too much water early in a run. In finance, I'm building wealth or financial security by resisting certain comforts or the latest gadgets and saving steadily over a long period of time.

There is no fast path. That information is best to learn now from me rather than wasting money on playing the lottery or getting suckered by a get-rich-quick scheme. If I run too fast down a hill, I risk an injury which would put me out of the race for a long period of time. If I invest in a get-rich-quick scheme and it fails, I will be delaying my long-term goals for several months or years depending on how expensive the scheme was.

Mr. Money Mustache, a pioneer in the FI space, says simply, "Live a less expensive life."

It's a mental game. Do I buy this *gadget* on Amazon or do I pay down debt and grow my savings? The gadget has a more immediate mental pull on us then a far-away savings goal. Right? Unless the far-away savings goal is also present in your everyday thinking. My long-term savings goal is ever present in my mind. My wife wanted new nightstands for our bedroom since we have never had "grown-up" furniture. She saw a nightstand she liked at Ethan Allen for $1,100 and showed it to me. I looked it over. It was very stylish, sleek, and had fully functioning drawers. Who wouldn't want it?

Spending over $1,000 for a nightstand wasn't an option. How did I convince my wife to come to my side?

I explained that we can certainly buy these beautiful Ethan Allen nightstands, but you will need to work an extra month right when you are ready to retire to afford it. I made my wife "own" the money decision, not me. If we are both rowing in the same direction, we will get there faster.

Lifestyle. Lifestyle. Lifestyle.

Are you able to take low-cost vacations and enjoy them? COVID-19 has everyone going camping. It's very inexpensive and fun! What about buying thrift clothes? Could you do it for part of your wardrobe? What about buying used gear on a site like GearTrade?[12] Can you make being frugal fun? I make it challenging. Can I find a stylish coffee mug at a garage sale for 25 cents?

Simply put, how you live today DIRECTLY AFFECTS how you live tomorrow. If you want to play the long game, then you must willingly choose to give up comfort today.

Opportunity costs.

Living frugally really helps me take a look at my thoughts and if I am putting too much weight on what other people think of me and my possessions. I like good gear, so buying a discounted Patagonia jacket may take me longer to achieve than just buying a brand new one. But in the end,

---

[12] https://www.geartrade.com

I'll save money and have the jacket I want. It just takes more time.

Someone told me that you have to choose either time or money. I'd rather take the extra time and invest my money.

I have learned that most lifestyles over-promise and under-deliver. If you look at your life in annual slices, what did you save this past year and what did you spend?

In our marriage, my wife and I remind each other of where we are going and where we have been! It's important to look back to see what behaviors got you to where you are today. What has worked and what mistakes do you wish you could correct? I am not proposing lingering in the past to beat yourself up, but reflecting on what has contributed to your wealth or perhaps delayed progress through debt, will aid you on the frugal road less traveled.

Are you surprised when you find out one of your neighbors is actually a millionaire? They drive used cars, have a modest house, and are industrious. If you had over a million dollars, would you buy a used car? Here's how they probably became a millionaire: They have been plodding along, living a modest lifestyle. Once you reach your goal,

Delayed Gratification

you just don't turn off the lifestyle. It becomes part of who you are.

Wealthy people think differently. They know that there is no substance behind buying a status symbol car, house, or other item. They also know that the neighbor down the street who bought the new car or boat or joined a club is probably highly leveraged and that any income is spent on immediate pleasures.

Who's the captain of my ship? Is it the shiny new car, fabulous new furniture, or cutting-edge piece of running gear? Or can I clearly envision my future life with no debt, savings goal attained, and freedom? I want the FREEDOM to do as I please. I try to steer towards freedom as often as possible.

I want to encourage you to be your own captain. Take control of your future. Ruminate on the disciplines outlined in this book and other motivating websites that point you into the direction of planning for your future and living a debt-free life.

Have you heard the phrase that states, "Building wealth is a negative art?"

Playing the long game is about the actions I don't take or the things I avoid. The hard part comes after I earn my money. The question is, "How am I avoiding the urge to spend it?"

As we all know, the world is screaming at us to spend NOW and pay LATER.

I make it a challenge to reuse or recycle items where I can. It helps the environment and your budget. Learn the art of negotiating when buying large-priced items. The vendor will still sell you the item even after you negotiate because the vendor is in the business of selling. You just don't know how low they will go. It doesn't hurt to ask. The worst they can do is sell it to you for the original price.

Do you think being frugal is a bad thing? Is it not hip? Is it not kind? Is it not generous? Can I be frugal and generous at the same time? Absolutely. We budget for charity and non-profit organizations that sync with our ideals and desires. I am the Captain of my finances and I tell my money where to be spent. As Dave Ramsey likes to say, "Every dollar has a name."

Marketing campaigns tell you to satisfy your wants, indulge yourself, and that you deserve it. Do I deserve it?

Delayed Gratification

Do I deserve to enjoy a new shiny object and delay my long-term savings goal? Playing the long game tells us just the opposite. Save NOW so you can SPEND later.

To borrow a tagline from the Libertarian Party – TANSTAAFL. It stands for, "There Ain't No Such Thing As A Free Lunch."

Everything has a price. There is no free ride. The government will not be funding your long-term savings goals.

When I was in college, I called it the "homework cloud." My buddies and I would go to a bar on a school night, shoot pool, listen to tunes and have a couple beers. But I never really had fun. I was trying to live in the moment even though I should have been doing my homework.

Whether they realize it or not, when people spend money they do not have, they also have a homework cloud hovering over them. They do not truly enjoy the purchase or experience because deep down they know the credit card statement is coming and they will have to pay.

I call this scenario the "Debt Cloud."

When one owes another person, they are the "borrower." Who owns who – the borrow or the lender? Debt is like a slave/master relationship. The borrower is the slave of the lender. Yuck! Who on Earth would willingly become a slave?

But that's exactly what's happening when people choose to live large today with tomorrow's money. They are walking into slavery and will have the "debt cloud" over them until they decide being debt-free is important enough to be an urgent goal.

Hope you enjoyed your vacation to Aruba? I know Visa did, or should I say, they are currently enjoying it.

Do you have the patience to build wealth or do you just want to avoid thinking about your future because it's too difficult? Maybe you are the type who has to get-rich-quick?

I suggested that the disciplines are easy to learn, but the truth is that they are extremely hard to implement. It really comes down to this: What price are you willing to pay?

Exercise:

- At what age do you think you'll be able to work until?

- Who will pay for your retirement? Can you rely on Social Security for your retirement funds?

Self-Reflection:

- What is holding you back from taking charge of your finances?
- Do you care what other people think of your house, car, job, clothes, or even the city you live in?
- What did you do with the last pay increase you received?

9

Final Lap

"Some things you miss because they're so tiny you overlook them. But some things you don't see because they're so huge."

- Robert M. Pirsig
Zen and the Art of Motorcycle Maintenance

When I cross the finish line, I am tired, thirsty and extremely satisfied that I completed the race. It feels good knowing I trained long and hard for the race and now I get to reap the reward.

What are treasure hunters looking for? It's obvious. They are looking for a hidden treasure that no one else can find. It takes a lot of resources and effort to launch an expedition and search for a hidden treasure.

Final Lap

Credit cards, the internet and sleek psychology-driven marketing campaigns are more of a recent phenomenon, but gambling has been among us for centuries.

I want to challenge you. Are you willing to gamble and see what the world wants to hand you in terms of your retirement savings and independent liberty? Or are you going to take hold of the steering wheel and become the captain you were designed to be?

You are the Captain, not your friends.

You are the Captain, not the new car salesmen.

You are the Captain, not the Google Ad.

You are the Captain, not Mr. MasterCard.

You are the Captain, not your employer.

If you don't accept your position as the Captain of your ship, many other false Captains are vying for the position. And boy can they be persuasive!

Hopefully I have shown you that true money management isn't about complicated math, but about your mindset.

Are you going to sit back and listen to the world…Buy NOW and pay LATER? Here are the choices: Slavery or freedom.

Running Your Finances

The world offers slavery while the disciplines outlined in this book offer freedom.

It's so amazing. It's really not about making a ton of money. It's about resisting the "wants" and having a daily plan. When new money comes into your month, continue your current lifestyle and determine to save the new net income.

You now have the tools to save and not spend your increase. Follow the disciplines: Set goals, take ownership, monitor your progress, hydrate regularly, find a support team, live below your means, take the slow road and delay gratification to play the long game.

When do you think the real race starts – your big race?

The gun goes off when you begin withdrawing your long-term reserves to live on during retirement. I hope your training schedule has prepared you to play the long game.

O Captain – what price are you willing to pay to attain your long-term savings goal?

Afterword

To continue your training before the big race starts, I encourage you to visit my blog for inspiration and coaching tips on playing the long game.

www.runningyourfinances.com

Let me know how your training is going.

Coach Jeffrey Sartori

About the Author

Jeffrey Sartori, born and raised in St. Louis MO, now lives as a Buckeye in Northeast Ohio with his wife and family. Jeffrey resides minutes away from the trails of the Cuyahoga Valley National Park, which fuel his running passion. It was on these trails that his love of running and personal finance intersected. Jeffrey enjoys teaching personal finance at the community level as well as coaching and mentoring on a corporate level. Jeffrey's history with mismanaging money, climbing out of debt, weathering a business failure and, finally, coming out wiser on the other side fuels his desire to coach and mentor others to play the long game.

Personal Stats (at the time of publication)

Running
13.1 PR= 1:35
10k PR= 40:16
Running Shoes = Topo Magnifly 3
Trail Shoes = Topo Ultraventure 2
Watch = Garmin Forerunner 35
Hydration Belt = Adalid

Asset Allocation – 85/10/5
75%   VFIAX   (Vanguard 500 Index Fund)
10%   VWILX (Vanguard International Growth Fund)
10%   VBILX   (Vanguard Intermediate-Term Bond Index Fund)
5%   Fundrise eREIT

Percent of Net Income (Gross Income minus Taxes) dedicated to long-term savings: 41%

Paid-Off Assets
Personal Home
2012 Honda Pilot (family car)
2010 Toyota Prius (commuter car)
2003 Toyota Camry (kid car)

Made in the USA
Coppell, TX
09 February 2023